KEYS TO GOOD GOVERNMENT

According to the Founding Fathers

DAVID BARTON

Aledo, Texas
www.wallbuilders.com

Additional materials available from:
WallBuilders
P.O. Box 397
Aledo, TX 76008
(817) 441-6044
www.wallbuilders.com

Cover Painting:
Washington Addressing the Constitutional Convention by Junius Brutus Stearns;
Courtesy, Virginia Museum of Fine Arts, Richmond. Gift of Colonel and
Mrs. Edgar W. Garbisch.

Cover Design:
Jeremiah Pent
Lincoln-Jackson
235 Wenner Way
Ft. Washington, PA 19034

Library of Congress Cataloging-in-Publication Data
342.029
Barton, David.
Keys to Good Government: According to the Founding Fathers.
Aledo, TX: WallBuilder Press
56 p.; 21 cm.
Endnotes included.
A transcript of the video and audio by the same title.
ISBN 10: 0-925279-36-6
ISBN 13: 978-0-925279-36-6
B291
1. U.S. – Politics and government   2. U.S. – Constitutional history   I. Title

Printed in the United States of America

Keys to Good Government

God has indeed blessed America. Under His Providence over the last two centuries, America has risen to levels and achievements attained by no other nation in the history of the world. Yet, ironically, in a nation once distinguished for its faith and made great by its people of faith, in recent years public expressions of that same faith have been viewed as a menace to society rather than an asset; and nowhere had this change been more evident than in the courts.

For example, in the case *Warsaw v. Tehachapi*, a federal court ruled that it was unconstitutional for a public cemetery to have a planter in the shape of a cross because – according to the court – if someone were to view that cross, it could cause emotional "distress" and thus constitute "injury-in-fact." [1]

In the case *Roberts v. Madigan*, a federal court ruled that a teacher at school could not be seen publicly with his own personal copy of the Bible, and then ruled that a classroom library containing 237 books must remove from the library the two books dealing with Christianity. [2]

In the case *Alexander v. Nacogdoches School District*, a member of the federal drug czar's office was prohibited from delivering an anti-drug message to students in a Texas school district. The court agreed that the speaker was indeed an anti-drug expert, admitting that he had already delivered his secular anti-drug message to over 3,000,000 students at thousands of public schools across the nation; but because the speaker was also publicly known as a Christian, he was therefore disqualified from speaking. [3]

In the case *Commonwealth v. Chambers*, a man was convicted and sentenced by a jury for taking an axe handle and brutally clubbing to death a 71-year-old woman in order to steal her Social Security check. The jury's sentence was overturned because the prosecuting attorney – in a statement that lasted less than five seconds – had mentioned a Bible verse in the courtroom. For mentioning seven words from the Bible in the courtroom, the court set aside the jury sentence of a man convicted of a brutal murder. [4]

Does that decision to overturn the jury's sentence represent good government? From a Biblical standpoint, the purpose of government is to reward the righteous and punish the wicked (c.f., I Timothy 1, I Peter 2, Romans 13, etc.), and this has long been the American policy; but in this case, the wicked was protected and the righteous was punished – a decision that violates every traditional standard for sound government.

Such egregious decisions (and others like them on issues ranging from private property protection to education, from environment to criminal justice) fuel the outcry for better government. Yet how to achieve good government has been the subject of debate for over three centuries in America, with differing conclusions reached on how to achieve that goal.

For example, in the 1660s when the people of Carolina were drafting their first constitution, they sought help from political philosopher John Locke. He authored their lengthy 1669 constitution [5] on the thesis that good government would be secured through the establishment of good laws. Locke reasoned that if righteous laws were embedded directly into the constitution, then no matter who was in office, he would always be bound by those righteous laws.

However, William Penn applied a dramatically different approach when he established the government of Pennsylvania under a short and brief governing document at about the same time. Penn believed that good laws were necessary, but he did not believe that a long constitution filled with righteous laws would be the means of securing good government. He explained that something more was necessary:

> Governments, like clocks, go from the motion men give them. . . . Wherefore governments rather depend upon men, than men upon governments. Let men be good and the government cannot be bad. . . . But if men be bad, the government [will] never [be] good. . . . I know some say,

"Let us have good laws, and no matter for the men that execute them." But let them consider that though good laws do well, good men do better; for good laws may [lack] good men... but good men will never [lack] good laws, nor [allow bad] ones. [6]

Penn argued that the soundness of government depended more upon the quality of leaders than the quality of laws – the same position set forth in Scriptures such as Proverbs 29:2, which declares:

> When the righteous rule, the people rejoice; when the wicked rule, the people groan.

Significantly, our Founding Fathers understood and embraced this approach – a fact demonstrated in the first governments they created.

Their opportunity to create those governments was the result of approving the Declaration of Independence. The day before they approved the separation from Great Britain, each of them had been a British citizen, living in a British colony, with thirteen crown-appointed British governors running the state governments. But by separating from Great Britain, they had effectively abolished their existing state governments. As a result, they returned home from Philadelphia to their own states and began creating new state constitutions to establish new state governments.

For example, Declaration signers Samuel Adams, John Hancock, Robert Treat Paine, and John Adams helped write Massachusetts' first constitution; signers Benjamin Franklin and James Smith helped write Pennsylvania's; William Paca, Charles Carroll, and Samuel Chase helped write Maryland's; George Read and Thomas McKean helped write Delaware's; etc.

Notice the governing philosophy incorporated in these documents – such as in the Delaware constitution:

> Every person, who shall be chosen a member of either house, or appointed to any office or place of trust . . . shall . . . make

and subscribe the following declaration, to wit: "I do profess faith in God the father, and in Jesus Christ, His only Son, and in the Holy Ghost, one God, blessed forevermore, and I do acknowledge the Holy Scriptures of the Old and New Testament to be given by divine inspiration." [7]

Today, this belief would be a desirable prerequisite for entering Christian seminaries; ironically, however, this was the Founders' requirement for leaders to enter politics. Notice, however, that the emphasis is on the quality of individual placed into office, not the quality of laws.

The other state constitutions reflected the same approach. For example, the Pennsylvania constitution declared:

And each member [of the legislature], before he takes his seat, shall make and subscribe the following declaration, viz: "I do believe in one God, the Creator and Governor of the universe, the rewarder of the good and the punisher of the wicked, and I do acknowledge the Scriptures of the Old and New Testament to be given by Divine Inspiration." [8]

The Massachusetts constitution likewise stipulated:

[All persons elected must] make and subscribe the following declaration, viz. "I do declare that I believe the Christian religion and have firm persuasion of its truth." [9]

North Carolina's constitution required that:

No person, who shall deny the being of God, or the truth of the [Christian] religion, or the divine authority either of the Old or New Testaments, or who shall hold religious principles incompatible with the freedom and safety of the State, shall be capable of holding any office, or place of trust or profit in the civil department, within this State. [10]

(Similar declarations can be found in other constitutions penned by our Founders.)

Significantly, the state constitutions written by the Founders followed the same general pattern: they established a republican form of government, delineated its general operations and scope of powers, included a bill of rights to protect individual liberties, and then focused on the types of individuals that would fill the offices and operate the form of government they had just created. This approach of focusing on the quality of leaders rather than of laws directly affected the length of those early documents in a manner strikingly different from contemporary ones.

For example, if individuals today were placed in the position of writing a new constitution for their state, the result might be similar to that found in some of the more recent (relatively speaking) constitutions of territories that entered the United States. For example, when Oklahoma became a state in 1907, its constitution was over 100 pages long; however, the average length of the constitutions created by the Founding Fathers was a mere five pages! (The same characteristic lengthiness is also visible in the constitutions of other twentieth-century states, including those of Arizona, New Mexico, Hawaii, Alaska, etc.)

The lesson was clear: the correct caliber of leader, joined to the right set of guiding principles (i.e., a republican form of government whose powers are specified in a written constitution, coupled with a list of inalienable rights not to be infringed by government), will produce the right kind of laws. Using this approach, those early American states became shining models of good government, and their example was emulated by nations across the world.

Having embedded these principles at the core of American government, our Founding Fathers went to great lengths to ensure that we would neither forget nor neglect these principles of sound governance. Seeking to transmit these principles to subsequent generations, many Founders became directly involved with education. In fact, in the ten years following the American Revolution, they established more colleges in America than in the 150 years preceding the Revolution; [11] they were indeed committed to transmitting sound principles from generation to generation.

Noah Webster was one of the many Founders who became directly involved in education. He served not only as a soldier during the Revolution but also as a legislator and a judge afterwards. He was one of the first to call for a Constitutional Convention and was personally responsible for language in Article 1, Section 8, of the Constitution. He helped establish Amherst College, became one of America's most prolific textbook writers, and was titled "Schoolmaster to America" for his profound contributions to education.

One of his famous texts used in public school classrooms for generations was his *History of the United States*. In it, he told students:

> When you become entitled to exercise the right of voting for public officers, let it be impressed on your mind that God commands you to choose for rulers, "just men who will rule in the fear of God." The preservation of [our] government depends on the faithful discharge of this duty; if the citizens neglect their duty and place unprincipled men in office, the government will soon be corrupted; laws will be made, not for the public good so much as for selfish or local purposes; corrupt or incompetent men will be appointed to execute the laws; the public revenues will be squandered on unworthy men; and the rights of the citizens will be violated or disregarded. [12]

While Webster's description of the ills of government sounds like a contemporary news account, what he described was not a widespread problem in his day; he was simply pointing out what _would_ occur if unprincipled, unGodly rulers were placed into office. Webster then concluded:

> If [our] government fails to secure public prosperity and happiness, it must be because the citizens neglect the divine commands and elect bad men to make and administer the laws. [13]

Although Webster warned that our form of government would not endure unless we kept God-fearing people of faith and character in office, doesn't the security of our government really depend more upon the people rather than their leaders? After all, aren't the people the most important element in a democracy?

This is part of our problem today: we think we are a democracy, but we are not. As evidence of this fact, recall that when we pledge allegiance to the American flag, we pledge allegiance to the republic – not the democracy – of the United States. America was founded as a republic, not a democracy; and while few today can define the difference between the two, there is a difference – a big difference.

A democracy is a form of government that has existed for millennia, and it was a form of government well known at the American Founding. Our Founding Fathers had an opportunity to establish a democracy and deliberately chose not to. They intentionally established America and each of the states as republican – not democratic – governments. In their minds, we were not, and were never to become a democracy. Confirming this, Bill of Rights framer Fisher Ames observed:

> A democracy is a volcano which conceals the fiery materials of its own destruction. These will produce an eruption, and carry desolation in their way. [14]

Declaration signer Benjamin Rush similarly noted:

> A simple democracy is the devil's own government. [15]

And John Adams also cautioned:

> Remember, democracy never lasts long. It soon wastes, exhausts, and murders itself. There never was a democracy yet that did not commit suicide. [16]

Numerous other Founders issued similar declarations condemning democracies and praising republics. In fact, they so strongly opposed democracy as a form of government that when they created the federal Constitution, they included language in Article 4, Section 4 requiring that "each state maintain a *republican* form of government."

The primary difference between a democracy and a republic is the fundamental source of its authority. In a democracy, the people are the highest source of authority; in America, however, there was a source of authority higher than the people, and it was that higher source which formed the basis of our government. As Noah Webster explained to students in a famous textbook:

> [O]ur citizens should early understand that the genuine source of correct republican principles is the Bible, particularly the New Testament, or the Christian religion. [17]

In a democracy, whatever the people desire is what becomes policy. Therefore, if a majority of the people decide that murder is no longer a crime, in a democracy, murder will no longer be a crime. However, not so in the American republic: in our republic, murder will always be a crime, for murder is always a crime in the Word of God. It is this immutable foundation that has given our republic such enduring stability, for since man at his core does not change, he continues to need the same restraints today that he needed when the Bible was written thousands of years ago. It is the rights and wrongs revealed in the Bible that have provided the moral and institutional standards for our republic.

Numerous early law books affirmed this, including Blackstone's *Commentaries on the Laws*. [18] Blackstone's principles formed the basis of American law from 1766 until 1920, and for decades, it was *the* final authority in the U. S. Supreme and lower courts. Blackstone's *Commentaries* (highly recommended by numerous famous Americans, including James Madison, James Wilson, John Marshall, Charles Finney, Abraham Lincoln, etc.), taught that human laws could not contradict God's direct decrees, and that only if God had *not* ruled in an area were men then free to set their own legislative policy. It explained:

> To instance in the case of murder: this is expressly forbidden by the divine. . . . If any human law should allow or enjoin us to commit it, we are bound to transgress that human law. . . .

But with regard to matters that are . . . not commanded or forbidden by [the Scriptures] – such, for instance, as exporting of wool into foreign countries – here the . . . legislature has scope and opportunity to interpose. [19]

God's Word also provided the basis for what are termed inalienable rights (rights bestowed by God on every individual, regardless of race, gender, or social station). Among man's inalienable rights were those of life, liberty, property, religious freedom, self-protection, due process, sanctity of the home, as well as others listed throughout the Declaration of Independence and the Bill of Rights.

Significantly, our founding documents directly acknowledge: (1) that God gave these rights to men ("all men . . . are endowed by their Creator with certain inalienable rights"), and (2) that it is the purpose of government to protect these rights ("to secure these rights, governments are instituted among men"). So crucial to the maintenance of America's republican government was the knowledge of God's standards and God-given rights, that Thomas Jefferson queried:

> [C]an the liberties of a nation be thought secure if we have removed their only firm basis – a conviction in the minds of the people that these liberties are the gift of God, that they are not to be violated but with His wrath? Indeed, I tremble for my country when I reflect that God is just – that His justice cannot sleep forever. [20]

Since the basis of our American republic rests on God's standards, the only way to preserve the nation's foundation is for citizens to have a knowledge of those standards and place into office individuals who both understand those standards and will protect America's foundation – that is, for citizens to choose leaders who recognize inalienable rights and will prevent government encroachment upon them.

It is for this reason that a republic is a much more difficult form of government to maintain than a democracy, for a republic requires more effort from the voters – not only must they understand their own government but they must also diligently investigate the beliefs of candidates before placing them into office. As John Adams explained:

> We electors have an important constitutional power placed in our hands: we have a check upon two branches of the legislature. . . . It becomes necessary to every [citizen] then, to be in some degree a statesman: and to examine and judge for himself . . . [the] political principles and measures. Let us examine them with a sober . . . Christian spirit. [21]

A democracy is the deterioration of a republic – it is a lazy man's form of government. It requires no effort and no research of candidates or long-term issues; it is simply based on what a majority of the people feel at a given time and is primarily motivated by emotions and selfishness – by what is best for "me" rather than what is best for others and for the country.

An excellent illustration of the inherent deficiencies of a democracy is seen in what transpired around Jesus during the final week of his life here on earth. As he entered Jerusalem, a great crowd ushered him in, seeking to make him their king; the next week, however, the same crowd shouted, "Kill the bum! Give us the thief Barabbas instead!" What a change – make Him king one week and kill Him the next! That is a democracy – it fluctuates in direct response to the variable feelings of the people, and its policies are based on what they want at any given instant. A democracy is what Founding Father Benjamin Rush aptly called a "mobocracy." [22]

Benjamin Rush was one of America's most influential Founding Fathers, signing the Declaration of Independence and serving in the presidential administrations of John Adams, Thomas Jefferson, and James Madison. Furthermore, he helped found five universities, authored numerous textbooks, and was one of the first Founders to call for free, national public schools. He understood the instability of a democracy; he also understood that if our people ever lost their knowledge of the Bible and its rights and wrongs, then we would lose our republican government. As he explained:

[T]he only means of establishing and perpetuating our republican forms of government . . . is the universal education of our youth in the principles of Christianity by means of the Bible. [23]

Regrettably, America has forgotten many of these principles of government and has moved away from what the Founders so clearly articulated. This seems amazing considering the lengths to which they went to ensure that we would always know and understand those principles. How did we forget? How did we depart from those teachings?

The movement away from those principles came as a result of destructive teachings introduced and widely disseminated during the last half of the nineteenth-century by men such as Colonel Robert Ingersoll, one of America's first openly avowed and proudly self-proclaimed militant secular humanists. He aggressively attacked both Judaism and Christianity in order to remove the Judeo-Christian ethic from America. He wanted a different religion to be the foundation of government, explaining:

> We are laying the foundations of the grand temple of the future . . . wherein . . . will be celebrated the religion of Humanity. . . . We are looking for the time when . . . REASON, throned upon the world's brain, shall be the King of Kings and God of Gods. [24]

Ingersoll advanced two teachings to help achieve that goal: (1) compartmentalizing the "religious" from the "secular," and (2) excluding a candidate's religious and moral beliefs from consideration of his competency for office (that is, to ignore a candidate's private life and character). Tragically, these two teachings, although revolutionary at the time, have now become widely accepted, even among many in the God-fearing community.

Concerning the latter teaching, Ingersoll asserted:

> The religious views of a candidate should be kept entirely out of sight. . . . All these things are private and personal. [25]

However, such a policy is illogical. That is, it might be advisable to separate a candidate's religious views from his run for office if citizens could be guaranteed that no public policy touching religion would ever arise while he was in office; but this has never happened and never will. In fact, in any given session of Congress today, from 10,000 to 13,000 bills are introduced, scores of which specifically address religious issues and values. The same is true at the state level (although fewer bills are introduced) and at the local level. Therefore, since a public official at every level of government will in some manner address religious issues, it is advisable to inquire into a candidate's personal religious views.

To ignore a candidate's religious views is as irrational as ignoring his economic views. It is certain that he will enact policy on economic issues, so it is important to know his economic views; the same is true with a candidate's religious views. Unfortunately, however, too many today separate a candidate's views on religious issues from his candidacy, fueling the notion that private life and views are irrelevant and have no bearing on professional public service.

Americans long believed that one's private life and beliefs were an important indicator of the type of leader a candidate would make. In fact, the conviction of this truth was so strong that for genera-tions it formed a core element in classroom instruction. One famous text incorporating this teaching was so popular that after being first published in December of 1800, it went through over 200 reprints, even being a favorite of President Abraham Lincoln. [26] That text taught students that they must always examine the private life and character of a leader, explaining:

> [P]ublic character . . . is no evidence of true greatness, for a public character is often an artificial one. [27]

The textbook illustrated the truth of this axiom with the example of Benedict Arnold. In his public capacity, Arnold was a General in the American Army, an early leader in the American Revolution, and a war hero in the momentous battle of Saratoga in 1777, with monuments having been erected to honor his military exploits.

However, during the same time that he was being publicly lauded as an American patriot, in private he was embezzling supplies destined for the starving troops at Valley Forge, selling the supplies on the black market, and then pocketing the profits – all while American soldiers were dying for lack of those supplies. So greedy was Arnold that he even betrayed West Point to the enemy for money. Clearly, he was a traitor to his country. So was his public life or his private life a better indicator of his true character? Obviously, his private life. The textbook thus concluded:

> It is not, then, in the glare of public, but in the shade of private life that we are to look for the man. Private life is always real life. Behind the curtain, where the eyes of the million are not upon him . . . there he will always be sure to act himself. Consequently, if he act greatly [in private], he must be great indeed. Hence it has been justly said that "Our private deeds, if noble, are noblest of our lives." . . . [I]t is the private virtues that lay the foundation of all human excellence. [28]

Schoolbooks long taught Americans to examine the private life; but from what source did they derive that teaching? From several sources, including experience and common sense, the Scriptures, and the Founding Fathers.

One Founder outspoken about this teaching was John Witherspoon, a signer of the Declaration who served on over 100 different committees in Congress. He was also the President of Princeton University and is considered the educational father of many Founding Fathers, having personally trained one U. S. President, one Vice-President, three Supreme Court Justices, thirteen Governors, and at least twenty Senators and thirty Congressmen – not to mention several Cabinet Members [29] (and this does not include the numerous individuals he trained for state, local, and municipal offices).

What did this prominent Founder teach his students that caused so many to rise to high levels of leadership? Among other things, Witherspoon taught them the three basic traits of an American patriot:

That he is the best friend to American liberty who is the most sincere and active in promoting true and undefiled religion, and who sets himself with the greatest firmness to bear down profanity and immorality of every kind. Whoever is an avowed enemy of God, I scruple not to call him an enemy to his country. [30]

According to Witherspoon, the first trait of an American patriot – the first indicator of a true leader – was that he be an active and sincere promoter of "true and undefiled religion." Second was that he "set himself with the greatest firmness to bear down profanity and immorality of every kind." Why would this trait be necessary for a good leader? Because with America's republican form of government, if the people became profane and immoral, then the government would also become profane and immoral; and since history proves that profane and immoral governments do not endure, then if someone loved America and its form of government, he would bear down on the enemies of good government: profanity and immorality. Witherspoon's third characteristic was that whoever was "an avowed enemy of God" was "an enemy to his country." Why? Since the American republic was firmly built on the principles of God's Word, if an individual opposed what God stood for, he opposed the very foundation on which America had been built. How, then, could he be a true patriot?

(Abigail Adams agreed with John Witherspoon, explaining: "[A] true patriot must be a religious man. . . . [H]e who neglects his duty to his Maker may well be expected to be deficient and insincere in his duty towards the public." [31])

Notice that two of Witherspoon's three characteristics focused on private life – one on private religious life, and one on private moral life. Private life was very important to the Founders. Therefore, the textbooks in part derived their teaching on private life from great leaders such as John Witherspoon; however, they also derived that teaching from the Bible.

One clear Biblical passage espousing this position was Matthew 7:16-20, in which Jesus explained that a tree's roots determined the character of its fruit – that if its root was corrupt, then its fruit would also be corrupt. As he reminded His listeners, grapes could not be picked from briar bushes, or figs gathered from thistle plants; what one was at his roots – at his core – would determine what eventually would manifest itself in public.

Nonetheless, many today absolutely refuse to consider one's "roots" – one's private life; they want to ignore private character and believe that the one they elect will somehow produce good results simply because he promised to do so during his campaign. This is an unsound approach, based on unrealistic, fanciful thinking. To find out if there will be good fruit in a leader, first examine his roots – his private life and character. As John Witherspoon explained:

> Those who wish well to the State ought to choose to places of trust men of inward principle, justified by exemplary conversation [lifestyle]. Is it reasonable to expect wisdom from the ignorant? fidelity [faithfulness] from the profligate [unfaithful]? assiduity [diligence] and application to public business from men of a dissipated [careless] life? Is it reasonable to commit the management of public revenue to one who hath wasted his own patrimony [inheritance]? Those, therefore, who pay no regard to religion and sobriety in the persons whom they send to the legislature of any State are guilty of the greatest absurdity and will soon pay dear for their folly. [32]

In short, to know what fruit an individual will produce, check his roots – don't expect public faithfulness from one who is privately unfaithful, or public frugality from one who is privately extravagant, etc. Always investigate a candidate's private religious and moral beliefs and behavior.

According to John Adams, it was the presence of private moral and religious beliefs that produced trustworthy public officials and thus provided a security for government and its citizens. In fact, in his diary entry for February 9, 1772, he discussed "that struggle which I believe always happens between virtue and ambition," insightfully noting that an individual in office who lacks virtue will "appl[y] himself to the passions and prejudices, the follies and vices of great men in order to obtain their smiles, esteem, and patronage, and consequently their favors and preferment." [33] This is an accurate description of what today may be termed a "politician" – an individual who willingly compromises principles in order to maintain favor with his party and constituents and thus win reelection. A statesman, however, will not compromise principles, regardless of the cost. What makes the difference between a politician and a statesman – what makes one willing to compromise principles and the other one not?

According to Adams, it was embracing the Biblical conviction of the reality of future rewards and punishments. That is, a statesman realizes that he will stand before God and account to Him for what he does in private as well as in public; this awareness of imminent accountability to God serves as a restraint on personal misbehavior. Such a restraint is especially important for office-holders, for although they are termed "public officials," most of what they do in their official capacities actually occurs in private. Therefore, if there is no self-imposed restraint on a public official's private actions stemming from a sense of his accountability to God, then that public official is a danger to good government because of the compromises he invariably will make.

Was John Adams a politician or a statesman? – was he willing to compromise principles, or was he determined to stand firm even though it might cost him the next election? Adams was definitely a statesman, explaining, "The duration of future punishment terrifies me." [34] Because he understood that he would answer to God for his every action, John Adams guarded his private behavior and carefully weighed his public policy decisions before God; as a result, his reputation for public integrity remains untarnished to this day.

Religious leaders also reminded citizens of the positive impact on public policy that resulted from a candidate's belief in future rewards and punishments. For example, in an 1803 sermon preached in the Connecticut Capitol building before Governor Jonathan Trumbull and the Connecticut legislature – a sermon preached at their request – the Reverend Matthias Burnet explained:

> [F]eeble . . . would be the best form of government . . . without a sense of religion and the terrors of the world to come. . . . [B]anish a sense of religion and the terrors of the world to come from society, and you . . . leave every man to do that which is right in his own eyes [Judges 21:25]. . . . But the man who does not believe in the Being and Providence of God, or is not actuated by the fear and awe of Him, has in many cases no bond or restraint upon his conduct and therefore is not fit to be trusted with a nation's weal [prosperity and happiness], which he will not scruple [hesitate] – whenever he can with impunity – to sacrifice to his lust or ambition. . . . Think not that men who acknowledge not the providence of God nor regard His laws will be uncorrupt in office. [35]

This truth was so clear to citizens and so firmly embraced by them, that when the possibility arose that a man might be elected to national office who was not God-fearing, it seriously alarmed the patriotic-minded. For example, on February 7, 1801, Abigail Adams wrote a letter to her sister discussing the upcoming presidential election between Aaron Burr, known to be an irreligious man, and Thomas Jefferson, who at that time was being portrayed not only as a non-believer but even as an atheist and an infidel. [36] Although that charge against Jefferson was later proved erroneous, it was nonetheless a frightening charge, for it meant that America apparently would be making a decision between two men who were not God-fearing. Dreading this possibility, Abigail wrote her sister:

> Never were a people placed in more difficult circumstances than the virtuous part of our countrymen are at the present crisis. I have turned, and turned, and overturned in my mind

at various times the merits and demerits of the two candidates. Long acquaintance, private friendship, and the full belief that the private character of [Jefferson] is much purer than [Burr] inclines me to [Jefferson]. . . . Have we any claim to the favor or protection of Providence when we have against warning admonition and advice chosen as our Chief Magistrate [President] a man who makes no pretensions to the belief of an all wise supreme Governor of the World ordering or directing or overruling the events which take place in it? . . . [I]f we ever saw a day of darkness, I fear this is one. [37]

Because our early leaders viewed having Godly leadership as being indispensable to the preservation of American government, Noah Webster instructed students:

> In selecting men for office, let principle be your guide. Regard not the particular sect or denomination of the candidate – look to his character. . . . It is alleged by men of loose principles, or defective views of the subject, that religion and morality are not necessary or important qualifications for public stations. [38]

Webster noted that those who alleged that religion and morality were not essential considerations for public office fell into one of two categories: either they themselves had loose principles, or they had defective views of the subject. He continued:

> [T]he Scriptures teach a different doctrine. They direct that rulers should be men "who rule in the fear of God, able men, such as fear God, men of truth, hating covetousness." [39]

Significantly, the specific qualifications for officeholders that Webster recommended to students came not from himself but from the Scriptures. Webster was simply quoting Exodus 18, wherein the people were instructed to choose out from among themselves "rulers of thousands, rulers of hundreds, rulers of fifties, and rulers of tens" – that is, that they were to have elections for federal (the "thousands"), state (the "hundreds"), county (the "fifties"), and local leaders (the "tens"). The people, having been told to have elections, were also specifically instructed to select rulers at each level who would rule in the fear of God, "able men, such as fear God, men of truth, hating covetousness" (v. 21).

Ministers also reminded citizens of this God-given duty – such as in the Rev. Matthias Burnet's 1803 sermon at the Connecticut Capitol building, when he admonished his hearers:

> [L]ook well to the characters and qualifications of those you elect and raise to office and places of trust. . . . [L]et the wise counsel of Jethro . . . be your guide. Choose ye out from among you "able men, such as fear God, men of truth and hating covetousness" [Exodus 18:21] and set them to rule over you. [40]

The Reverend Chandler Robbins used the same Scripture in a 1791 sermon delivered in the Massachusetts Capitol building before Governor John Hancock, Lieutenant Governor Samuel Adams, and the Massachusetts legislature – a sermon delivered at their request. He similarly instructed his listeners:

> How constantly do we find it inculcated in the sacred writings, that rulers be "just men – fearers of God – haters of covetousness" [Exodus 18:21]. That they "shake their hands from holding bribes" [Isaiah 33:15], because, "a gift blindeth the eyes of the wise, and perverteth the words of the righteous" [Exodus 23:8]. [41]

Ministers, statesmen, and educators all pointed citizens toward the character qualifications that God Himself had set forth in the Scriptures. They also pointed out that there were consequences to ignoring this standard – as when Noah Webster told students:

> [I]t is to the neglect of this rule of conduct in our citizens [that is, of not selecting God-fearing leaders], that we must ascribe the multiplied frauds, breaches of trust, peculations and embezzlements of public property which astonish even ourselves, which tarnish the character of our country, which disgrace a republican government. [42]

Having noted the negative consequences that would result from ignoring the character of our leaders, Webster then concluded:

> When a citizen gives his suffrage [vote] to a man of known immorality, he abuses his trust [civic responsibility]; he sacrifices not only his own interest but that of his neighbor; he betrays the interest of his country. [43]

Webster asserted that if someone knowingly helped place an immoral person into office that he was a traitor to his country. Why? Because installing immorality and deficient character in office was the very thing that would destroy that office in particular and good government in general, thus making that voter an accessory to any destructive acts and policies enacted by that leader.

The Founding Fathers, school textbooks, and the Bible all taught Americans never to separate the private from the public, yet we began to accept otherwise, we started moving away from the principles of sound government that had been transmitted to us through the collective wisdom of previous generations and centuries.

Recall that Ingersoll, in addition to advocating that one's private life and views be divorced from qualifications for public office, also urged that religion be compartmentalized – that its influence and activities be limited to inside the four walls of the church and never touch the public arena. To support this proposition, Ingersoll asserted:

> Our government should be kept entirely and purely secular. . . . So our fathers said: "We shall form a secular government. . . ." The Declaration of Independence . . . denied the authority of any and all gods. . . . [They] agreed that there should be only one religion . . . and that was the religion of patriotism. Our fathers founded the first secular government that was ever founded in this world. [44]

Ingersoll's claim is, of course, blatantly and demonstrably false – including by the specific wording of the Declaration of Independence itself, which openly acknowledges God in four separate locations, therefore directly repudiating his claim that "the Declaration of Independence... denied the authority of any and all gods." (Numerous official writings and acts of the Founding Fathers also repudiate Ingersoll's claim.) Nevertheless, Ingersoll had effectively introduced the concept that religious people and principles had nothing to do with government. He (and many others, including an organization formed in 1876 known as the National Liberal League [45]) began to pursue the compartmentalization of religion – that religion and people of faith should be placed into compartments separate from public, educational, and governmental arenas.

Slowly, the church acquiesced to this heretical teaching of compartmentalization and even gradually began to relinquish the role of moral conscience and ethical influence that it had exercised for centuries. Instead, it began to encourage its children to enter so-called "spiritual" arenas such as the ministry or missionary work but to avoid so-called "secular" professions such as science, education, media, law, or politics. In essence, the church determined that it no longer would be salt and light throughout society, but rather just inside the church.

The church and people of faith have now so separated themselves from civil society that they largely do not even participate in something as simple as voting. Less than half the Christian community now votes even in presidential elections – and this is when voter turnout is normally the highest; regrettably, the numbers are even lower in non-presidential elections [46] and lower still in local elections. Christians seem to have lost the concept of individual civic stewardship they once so strongly embraced – the concept that Christian leaders such as Benjamin Rush had so clearly articulated:

> [E]very citizen of a republic. . . . must watch for the state as
> if its liberties depended upon his vigilance alone. [47]

That statement accurately described the responsibility that Americans – especially God-fearing ones – once felt for maintaining good government. Not only were we once well-informed voters, we were active voters as well. For example, when Daniel Webster ran for the

U. S. House in 1824, there was a one-hundred percent voter turnout in that election; and of 5,000 eligible voters, Daniel Webster himself received 4,990 of the votes. [48]

Removing ourselves from the civic and political arenas not only violates historical precedent but it also ignores what America's early church leaders taught. For example, Charles Finney – a prominent minister and leader in America's Second Great Awakening in the early 1800s – warned:

> [T]he time has come that Christians must vote for honest men and take consistent ground in politics. . . . Christians have been exceedingly guilty in this matter. But the time has come when they must act differently. . . . God cannot sustain this free and blessed country which we love and pray for unless the Church will take right ground. . . . It seems sometimes as if the foundations of the nation are becoming rotten, and Christians seem to act as if they think God does not see what they do in politics. But I tell you He does see it, and He will bless or curse this nation according to the course [Christians] take. [49]

In recent years, the God-fearing religious community has not upheld its responsibilities as voters. Where we currently find ourselves is best expressed by President James A. Garfield, himself a Christian minister, who – on the centennial celebration of America – explained:

> [N]ow, more than ever before, the people are responsible for the character of their Congress. If that body be ignorant, reckless, and corrupt, it is because the people tolerate ignorance, recklessness, and corruption. If it be intelligent, brave, and pure, it is because the people demand these high qualities to represent them in the national legislature. . . . [I]f the next centennial does not find us a great nation . . . it will be because those who represent the enterprise, the culture, and the morality of the nation [i.e., God-fearing citizens] do not aid in controlling the political forces. [50]

What we see in our elected officials – whether praiseworthy or culpable – reflects our own actions (or lack thereof) as citizens. And although there are many exemplary public officials in office today, by our negligence and lack of investigation into the private religious and moral beliefs of candidates, the nation has become plagued with an increasing number of corrupt officials.

In fact, the *Statistical Abstract of the United States* now documents the harmful aftermath of embracing the two aberrant teachings of compartmentalization and of ignoring a candidate's private life. The *Statistical Abstract*, published annually by the federal government, sets forth statistics from the various cabinet level departments, and the appearance of a new category in the *Statistical Abstract* always heralds the emergence of a new national problem.

For example, it was not until 1976 that the category on sexual abuse of children first appeared. While the crime has always existed, prior to 1976 it occurred so infrequently that it did not warrant individual monitoring; but by 1976, so many police reports on this crime were being filed that a serious effort was made to ascertain the scope of the problem. When tracking began in 1976, the rate of sexual abuse of children was already too high, with three cases for each 10,000 children; but within only a decade, the problem had increased by almost 500 percent. [51] Nevertheless, it was the *Statistical Abstract* that first heralded the emergence of this new national problem.

Similarly, the recording of AIDS cases did not begin until 1981. At that time, 199 cases of AIDS had been reported – enough to warrant attention as a serious problem. Today, there are almost 40,000 new cases each year, with half-a-million having died from AIDS and nearly half-a-million more currently living with it – an increase of over 5,000 percent from that original reporting. [52] Again, the *Statistical Abstract* first recorded the emergence of AIDS as a new national problem.

Interestingly, federal prosecutions of public corruption did not appear as a category in the *Statistical Abstract* until 1973. At that time, 244 cases of alleged public corruption were reported – enough to indicate a serious national problem and a disturbing trend among public officials. However, within a few short decades, the number had increased by nearly 400 percent to more than 1,200 cases. [53] This rapid increase in public corruption should come as no surprise, however, since (1) voters had been discouraged from examining a candidate's roots and (2) so many people of faith voluntarily compartmentalized themselves from the political process. They evidently forgot that good government was the result of good leaders, and that good leaders had to be elected by good people.

Not surprisingly, embracing these two destructive teachings resulted in a change not only in the quality of our leaders but also a change in their philosophy and worldview. And logically so, for when God-fearing individuals depart any arena, their values depart with them; and when ungodly individuals enter an arena, their values enter with them. The result is that many offices are now filled with leaders who are not God-fearing and who therefore have no respect for traditional religious and moral values. A vivid illustration of this truth is readily apparent in a short review of the U. S. Supreme Court's decisions on specific issues.

For example, voluntary school prayer had been permitted in America's public schools for over three centuries, and had been constitutional for 171 consecutive years under the Constitution before the Court struck down that practice in 1962. Why had voluntary school prayer remained constitutional for 171 consecutive years? Because voluntary prayer had been laudable in the personal beliefs of the Founding Fathers originally placed on the Court as well as in the beliefs of subsequent Justices who filled their places. But by the 1960s, a new group had been seated on the Court with a different set of personal values. They seized a statement that suited their personal beliefs – a misleading phrase found neither in the Constitution, the First Amendment, nor any other official founding document ("separation of church and state"). Under those Justices' distorted application of that two-centuries-old phrase, in the case *Engel v. Vitale*, [54] voluntary school prayer was suddenly and without precedent [55] deemed to be improper.

The next year, the Court struck down another long-standing practice – a practice specifically implemented by Founding Fathers such as Benjamin Rush, Noah Webster, Samuel Adams, John Adams, Jedidiah Morse, William Samuel Johnson, Benjamin Franklin, Fisher Ames, Francis Hopkinson, John Witherspoon, Abraham Baldwin, and numbers of others. What was that practice? The use of the Bible in schools. [56]

On what ground did the Court order the removal of the Bible from education? One need only read the written opinion in that case (available either online or at any local county law library) to answer this question. In reaching its decision, the lower court had relied on the testimony of a psychologist who explained the danger of reading the Bible in schools, and the Supreme Court then repeated that testimony in its decision, reporting:

> [I]f portions of the New Testament were read without explanation, they could be and . . . had been psychologically harmful to the [student]. [57]

What an amazing pronouncement by the Court: the New Testament causes psychological damage – it causes brain damage to students! This statement was not a reflection of law or history; rather, it was a statement reflecting the beliefs of the Justices who issued that ruling. Consider: is it likely that God-fearing individuals would have declared that the Bible caused psychological harm? Hardly. Why? Because God-fearing individuals do not believe that.

Yet, the Court was not finished enacting its personal beliefs, for in the case *Stone v. Graham*, [58] it even ruled that it was unconstitutional for students at school voluntarily to see a copy of the Ten Commandments. That ruling was amazing, for a picture of Moses holding the Ten Commandments is actually etched in stone inside the Supreme Court, and depictions of the Ten Commandments appear in numerous locations throughout the Court building. Yet, the Court held that it was unconstitutional for students to see what appeared inside the Supreme Court building – one of America's most public structures!

Significantly, the Ten Commandments are found in hundreds of civic buildings, courthouses, and legislatures across the nation. In fact, one is more likely to find the Ten Commandments displayed in a government building than a church building. Why? Because for over two thousand years, the Ten Commandments have been recognized as the basis of civil law in the Western World – it is from the Ten Commandments that we derive laws against murder, theft, perjury, etc. Furthermore, courts have cited the Ten Commandments as an authority in dozens of cases over the past two centuries. [59] Neverthe-less, the Supreme Court ruled that students could no longer see the laws that formed the basis of our current civil laws because:

> If the posted copies of the Ten Commandments are to have any effect at all, it will be to induce the school children to read, meditate upon, perhaps to venerate and obey, the Command-ments. . . . [This] is not . . . permissible. [60]

Amazing! Students can't be allowed to see the Ten Commandments, for they might obey religious teachings at school – things like "Don't steal" and "Don't murder." Rarely has such anti-religious bias been so visibly manifest, yet that bias accurately reflected the beliefs of the Justices who made that decision.

The same personal bias of a judge against the Ten Command-ments was evidenced in a Florida courtroom where a man was on trial, accused of the brutal first-degree murder of his four-year-old stepdaughter. In that courthouse – as in so many others – the Ten Commandments hung on the wall. However, the judge ordered that the Ten Commandments be covered during the trial for fear that jurors would be prejudiced against the defendant if they saw the command, "Do not murder." [61] Yet, if jurors aren't to see the law that forbids murder, then why was the man even on trial?

The reasoning behind the Court's decisions in the voluntary prayer case, the Bible reading case, the Ten Commandments case, and other similar cases provide convincing evidence that leaders will rule by what they personally believe. All public policies – whether sound or ludicrous, whether from the judicial, legislative, or executive branch – will always reflect the personal ideas and beliefs of the public officials making those decisions.

Obviously, public policies directly affect the individual citizens who are the intended objects of those policies (such as the defendant in the Florida courtroom). However, public policies also have a direct impact on the entire city, state, or nation in which a policy is implemented, for just as God holds individuals accountable for what they do, He also holds communities, states, and nations accountable for what is done by their public officials. As the Reverend Chandler Robbins reminded the Massachusetts legislature in 1791:

> The Supreme Governor of the World rewards or punishes nations and civil communities only in this life. . . . [Political bodies] have no existence as such but in the present state; consequently, [they] are incapable of punishments or rewards in a future. We can conceive no way in which the divine Being shall therefore manifest the purity of his nature . . . towards such societies but by rewarding or punishing them here according to their public conduct [i.e., their public policies]. [62]

George Mason – the Father of the Bill of Rights – had previously affirmed that God judged communities for the public stands and policies of their political leaders. On the floor of the Constitutional Convention in 1787, he reminded delegates that:

> As nations cannot be rewarded or punished in the next world, so they must be in this. By an inevitable chain of causes and effects, Providence punishes national sins by national calamities. [63]

When fellow delegate Luther Martin returned home from the Constitutional Convention in Philadelphia, he reminded officials in his state of the same message:

> It was said – it ought to be considered – that national crimes can only be, and frequently are, punished in this world by national punishments. [64]

Because God blessed or cursed nations, states, or communities based on the policy positions taken by each, it was vital to place at the helm of government individuals who would take stands that God could honor and bless, thus causing the entire nation, state, or community (and those within it) to be blessed. As President George Washington reminded Americans in his "Inaugural Address":

> [T]he propitious [favorable] smiles of Heaven can never be expected on a nation that disregards the eternal rules of order and right which Heaven itself has ordained. [65]

Regrettably, in recent decades, the three branches of government from the federal to the local level have too often been filled with public officials who are politicians rather than statesmen – with individuals whose personal belief systems have not merely disregarded but have even countermanded "the eternal rules of order and right which Heaven itself has ordained." When those rules are disregarded by leaders, all citizens pay the price – a truth now affirmed statistically.

For example, following the 1962-1963 court mandate that religious principles be separated from students and official public venues, violent crime skyrocketed almost 700 percent. [66] Not surprisingly, funding for prisons also skyrocketed and is now one of the fastest-growing expenditures for state government; [67] states simply cannot build prisons fast enough to house all the criminal offenders. And despite the fact that school students are responsible for twenty percent of all crimes [68] and that half of all violent crimes, murders, and robberies are committed by youth aged 24 and below, [69] the Court nevertheless holds that these youth should not see things like "Don't steal" and "Don't kill" for fear that they might obey those "religious" teachings. Nine Justices made the original decision but the entire nation now pays the price both economically and in the destroyed lives of crime victims and offenders.

Further evidence of a significant statistical decline following the Court's religion-hostile policies is seen in moral measurements of youth. For example, following extended years of low rates:

- Birth rates for junior-high girls 10-14 years-old increased 460 percent [70]
- Sexual activity among fifteen year-olds skyrocketed [71]
- The percentage of teen births to unmarried women soared over 400 percent [72]
- The United States now has the highest teen pregnancy rate in the industrialized world [73]
- Sexually transmitted diseases among students also reached previously unrecorded levels [74]

Virtually every moral measurement kept by federal cabinet-level agencies reflects the same statistical pattern: the policies removing religious principles from the public sphere were accompanied by a corresponding decline in public morality. [75]

Very simply, officials who enact policies violating what George Washington called "the eternal rules of order and right which Heaven itself has ordained" harm the entire community under their influence. Yet, despite the obvious negative effects following the Court's various decisions, the Court cannot be held totally at fault for what has occurred. Who else is at fault?

The answer is provided in a parable wherein Jesus describes a man who had a good field, growing a good crop. That man awakened one morning and discovered that his crop was filled with tares and weeds. How did it happen that his field went from producing good to also producing bad? In Matthew 13:25, Jesus provided the answer, explaining that while the good men slept, the enemy came in and planted the tares. Significantly, Jesus did not fault the enemy for doing what he did; the problem was that the good men went to sleep. This is what has happened in America: too many of the good people have gone to sleep concerning their stewardship of government, embracing an apathy that results in ruin. As signer of the Constitution John Dickinson warned:

[Political] slavery is ever preceded by sleep. [76]

Incontrovertibly, much of the blame for the condition of America rests on the shoulders of the "good men" – the church and people of faith who went to sleep, thus allowing the enemy to enter and sow his tares.

What is the solution to reversing the negative trends of recent years? Jeremiah 6:16 instructs that if one wants the ways of peace and bounty, he should go back to the old paths. What were some of the "old paths"? Consider what was taught by early leaders such as John Jay, not only the president of the American Bible Society and the original Chief Justice of the U. S. Supreme Court but also one of the three Founders most responsible for the ratification and adoption of the Constitution. Jay directed:

> Providence has given to our people the choice of their rulers, and it is the duty (as well as the privilege and interest) of our Christian nation to select and prefer Christians for their rulers. [77]

Jay's statement is concise, but even more important than the statement is the reason he believed it important to keep Godly, God-fearing people of faith in office. Jay penned that statement in response to a letter written him by the Rev. Dr. Jedidiah Morse, one of America's leading theologians and educators (called the "Father of American Geography"). Morse had inquired of the Chief Justice whether it were permissible for a Godly person to vote for an ungodly candidate, to which Jay had replied:

> [This] is a question which merits more consideration than it seems yet to have generally received, either from the clergy or the laity. It appears to me that what the prophet said to Jehoshaphat about his attachment to Ahab affords a salutary lesson. [78]

Jay's reference was to the account in II Chronicles 19 involving King Ahab of Israel and King Jehoshaphat of Judah. Wicked King Ahab corresponded with righteous King Jehoshaphat and requested his help to fight an enemy. Righteous King Jehoshaphat agreed and made an alliance with wicked King Ahab. Together, they went off to fight Ahab's enemy at Ramoth-Gilead. After the battle, King Jehoshaphat returned home, where God sent a prophet to rebuke him for making an alliance with the wicked. The prophet's statement in verse 2 of that chapter was not only God's response to King Jehoshaphat but it was also John Jay's answer to the question of whether the Godly could vote for the ungodly:

> And Jehu the seer [the prophet], the son of Hanani, went out to meet him, and said to King Jehoshaphat, "Should you help the wicked, and love those who hate the Lord? Because of this, the wrath of the Lord is upon you." [79]

Jay's application of this Scriptural principle to voting was self-evident: if you helped place ungodly leaders in office (that is, if you made an alliance with the wicked through your vote), then you therefore had helped place ungodly principles in office; since God could not bless ungodly principles, how could God bless you for helping place those ungodly principles in office? However, if you placed Godly leaders in office, then you were placing Godly principles in office; since God could bless Godly principles, He therefore could bless you for helping place Godly principles in office.

Founders such as John Jay not only understood the mandate to elect God-fearing leaders, they also understood a truth that we are just beginning to grasp: no institution has intrinsic, inherent value – no institution is of itself either good or bad. For example, although many complain about the media and how biased it is, there is absolutely nothing wrong with the institution of the media. If the media is biased and has an ungodly agenda, it is because the people involved in the media have the wrong values. Similarly, if government is bad, it is because the people involved in government also have the wrong values. The simple fact is that institutions (whether government, law, media, education, entertainment, medicine, business, etc.) are much like cars – they take on the nature of whoever is behind the wheel – they simply reflect the values of those involved in them. This is why the Founders placed such an emphasis on the type and quality of people placed into office.

Moreover, Jay's statement about electing Godly individuals clearly requires political involvement – something that the church has come to dislike over the last half century. Yet, many of the Founding Fathers did not particularly like politics, especially partisan politics.

As an indication, consider an unequivocal declaration made by George Washington in his "Farewell Address" (considered to be the most significant political speech ever delivered by a U. S. President). In that address, Washington offered nearly a dozen warnings designed to keep America on track, including exposing what he described as America's "worst enemy." (Significantly, Washington spent forty-five years of his life fighting America's enemies; he knew an enemy when he saw one.) So what did Washington consider America's "worst enemy"? He explained:

> Let me . . . warn you in the most solemn manner against the baneful effects of the spirit of party. . . . It exists . . . in all governments . . . and is truly their <u>worst enemy</u>. The alternate domination of one [party] over another, sharpened by the spirit of revenge natural to party dissension . . . is itself a frightful despotism. . . . [T]he common and continual mischiefs of the spirit of party are sufficient to make it the interest and duty of a wise people to discourage and restrain it. [80] (emphasis added)

Don't misunderstand. Washington was <u>not</u> saying to abolish political parties, for parties *are* necessary; he was saying to abolish the *spirit* of party that places party interests and a love for that party above the country's interests and a love for the country. Political parties *are* necessary, for they are the mechanisms by which candidates are offered to the public; but recall that a party is simply an institution – it has no value of its own but simply takes on the nature of those involved in it.

Therefore, God-fearing people of faith should be actively involved in a political party: (1) to help select its candidates, (2) to vote in party primaries and help Godly candidates in that party advance so that the community will then have the best possible selection in the general election, and (3) to influence and help shape their party's platform (a platform sets forth a political party's public policy positions) and their party's rules (the rules are the self-imposed standards governing a party's internal operations). While voter turnout is low in general elections, it is even lower in primary elections; but because of that, a God-fearing citizen can actually have a greater influence on public policy by being active in the primaries of a party, for his vote will have greater impact.

When voting in a primary, your vote is confined to a specific party; therefore, vote for the candidate in that party who best conforms to Exodus 18:21 ("an able man, such as fears God, a man of truth, hating covetousness"). However, when voting later in the general election, don't vote solely on the basis of party, regardless of the particular party with which you might affiliate. There may well be a candidate in the other party who is more Godly than the candidate offered by your party, and thus better for the community, state, or nation. Always examine the values of *each* candidate running, regardless of party affiliation. (A number of voter web sites are available to help identify the specific beliefs of candidates on numbers of important issues, especially those related to Biblical values. Links to several such web sites are available at www.wallbuilders.com.) In short, an inordinate loyalty to a party is always to be discouraged, but a loyalty to proper principles – no matter the party in which they appear is always to be strongly encouraged.

Founder Benjamin Rush demonstrated this approach to politics. Recall that he was not only a member of the Continental Congress who signed the Declaration of Independence but he also served in the presidential administrations of John Adams, Thomas Jefferson, and James Madison. What makes this latter accomplishment so amazing is that each of those three presidents was from a different political party. (Although the dominant political parties at the time were the Federalists and the Anti-Federalists, there were also others, including the Whigs, Tories, Democrats, Aristocrats, etc.). How could Benjamin Rush serve for three presidents from three different political parties? What was his own party affiliation? He explained:

> I have been alternately called an Aristocrat and a Democrat. I am . . . neither. I am a Christocrat. [81]

He continued:

> I believe all power . . . will always fail of producing order and happiness in the hands of man. He alone Who created and redeemed man is qualified to govern him. [82]

Very simply, Benjamin Rush didn't care what the party called itself; he was focused on Biblical principles (i.e., he was a Christ-ocrat). When he found someone who stood for God's principles, he would stand with him, no matter the party. That lesson is still applicable today: the love of correct principles rather than the love of a party must be the key to our political involvement.

However, many Christians and God-fearing people of faith, having become accustomed to religious freedom in America, unwisely assert that they do not need to be politically involved because their rights come from God, not the government. What these individuals fail to recognize is that while our rights are indeed Biblically-given, they must be politically protected.

The fact that America has always provided the political protection to exercise our God-given rights (a protection lacking in most other nations) is what has made America so unique for so long. Americans have enjoyed freedoms unknown in the rest of the world because we long kept leaders in office who knew our God-given rights and provided political protection for the exercise of those rights. Yet, with the falling involvement of Christians and the commensurate increase of leaders who do not respect God-given rights, many citizens today are completely unaware of the current challenges to the most basic of their religious beliefs and practices. In fact, the question of whether Christians could even hand out Gospel material in public reached all the way to the U. S. Supreme Court! [83]

A number of other long-standing religious rights have also been recently challenged and taken to court, including whether individuals may:

- wear clothing with Christian messages [84]
- wear jewelry with a Christian cross [85]
- have a Bible study in their own college dorm rooms [86]
- pray privately, after work hours [87]
- share a book of Bible stories with someone else riding the bus with them [88]
- have prayer meetings [89] or Bible studies and religious gatherings in their own homes [90]
- pray prayers reflecting their own faith and use the word "Jesus" in public [91]

Concerning the once inalienable rights of churches, cases have now been filed challenging whether churches and other religious bodies may:

- require their staff to abide by Biblical standards of morality [92]
- follow Matthew 18:15 in dealing with church members [93]
- hire their own seminary professors, select curriculum reflecting their particular theology, and issue seminary degrees in accordance with their church beliefs, or whether the state must pre-approve their staff, curriculum content, and conferring of degrees [94]
- have food pantry ministries, [95] radio ministries, [96] homeless ministries, [97] Christian schools, [98] ministries to help non-violent criminals get back on track after their release from prison, [99] ministries to help those with chemical or alcohol dependencies [100]
- expand their facilities on their own property [101]

Concerning the rights of students, cases have been filed challenging whether students may:

- draw art posters with a picture of Jesus in them during kindergarten class [102]
- write a research report about Jesus [103]
- receive a Bible as a gift while at school [104]
- give their friends literature with religious references [105]
- invite their friends to religious meetings [106]

Additionally, cases have been filed challenging whether:

- cities may eliminate all churches through enacting "church-free zones" or prevent churches from entering the town [107]
- a paid advertisement may contain a religious message [108]
- a rancher may have a worship service in his own barn, located in the middle of his large ranch [109]
- sidewalk preaching may occur in public areas [110]
- and dozens of other similar issues.

It is shocking that such basic rights are now objects of legal challenge, but it simply confirms that if citizens desire to exercise their God-given rights without penalty, they must have political protection to do so – they must elect leaders and judges who embrace God-fearing values and will protect God-given rights.

An historical illustration of this principle is provided by two brothers during the American Revolution: John Peter Muhlenberg and Frederick Augustus Muhlenberg. Both were ordained ministers and pastors of congregations; Peter pastored in Virginia, and Frederick pastored in New York. On January 21, 1776, Peter preached to his Virginia congregation concerning the crisis then facing America, recounting to them the history of how America had been founded in pursuit of religious and civil liberties and that they were now in danger of losing those liberties. He then concluded with these words:

[I]n the language of holy writ [Ecclesiastes 3], there [is] a time for all things, a time to preach and a time to pray, but those times have passed away. [111]

Then, in a loud voice, he quoted from verse 8, announcing:

[T]here [is] a time to fight – and that time has now come! [112]

His sermon finished, he offered the benediction and then deliberately disrobed in front of the congregation, revealing the uniform of a military officer that he was wearing beneath his clerical robes. He descended from the pulpit, marched to the back door of the church, and ordered the drums to beat for recruits. Nearly three hundred men joined him there, and they became the Eighth Virginia Regiment. [113] Pastor John Peter Muhlenberg went on to become one of the highest-ranking officers in the American Revolution, finishing as a Major General under Commander-in-Chief George Washington. (It was not unusual for ministers to be involved in this manner; numbers of religious leaders became involved in the American Revolution simply to protect their civil and religious liberties. [114])

Significantly, Frederick strongly opposed what his brother Peter had done, and rebuked him in a manner and with words that could have been delivered in this modern era. He chided Peter:

You would have acted for the best if you had kept out of this business from the beginning. . . . I now give you my thoughts in brief – I think you are wrong in trying to be both soldier and preacher together. [115]

However, Peter responded with some strong thoughts of his own:

I am a clergyman – it is true; but I am a member of society as well as the poorest layman, and my liberty is as dear to me as to any man. Shall I then sit still . . . ? Heaven forbid it. . . . I am convinced it is my duty so to do and duty I owe to God and my Country. [116]

Peter understood that if he did not get involved, then he could not protect the rights important to him.

Conversely, Frederick believed that his right to be a pastor and guide and direct his church was secure without the need for outside involvement; after all, his rights had long been protected under both American and British policy. Nevertheless, when the British arrived in New York City in 1777, they drove Frederick from his church and desecrated the building. Frederick thus found himself rethinking his position, and like his brother, he, too, made the decision to get involved. He became a member of the Continental Congress and went on to become the original Speaker of the U. S. House of Representatives in the first federal Congress. Significantly, the signature of this ordained minister and pastor is one of only two on the Bill of Rights – the document in which he was striving to secure political protections for our God-given religious freedoms.

Very simply, not only does history repeatedly affirm that God-fearing leaders will protect God-given rights but also that public policies will reflect the values of those making the policies more than the values of the documents under which the policies are made. In fact, at the Constitutional Convention, John Francis Mercer succinctly explained:

> It is a great mistake to suppose that the paper we are to propose will govern the United States. [117]

That is, Mercer and the other Framers understood that it was a major error to believe that the Constitution would govern America. He correctly observed that it would be not the Constitution that would govern America but rather . . .

> it is the men whom it [the Constitution] will bring into the government, and the interest [they have] in maintaining it that are to govern them. The paper [i.e., the Constitution] will only mark out the mode and the form. Men are the substance and must do the business. [118]

Officials in all three branches swear an oath to uphold the Constitution, but the reality is that the acts proceeding from each branch will more accurately reflect the values of those involved in that branch than the values of the Constitution (or any other governing document).

For this reason, Christians and God-fearing people of faith must be involved in government, and – as all others do – they must carry their values with them, for this is what allows our government to operate as efficiently as it was intended. As John Adams reminded citizens:

> Our Constitution was made only for a moral and religious people. It is wholly inadequate to the government of any other. [119]

Consequently, we must elect individuals who embrace the timeless Biblical values so important to both the proper operation of our constitutional republic and our own future as a nation. Understanding this, the Rev. Charles Finney strongly admonished God-fearing citizens in his day:

> The church must take right ground in regard to politics. . . . Politics are a part of a religion in such a country as this, and Christians must do their duty to the country as part of their duty to God. . . . [God] will bless or curse this nation according to the course [Christians] take [in politics]. [120]

The Reverend Matthias Burnet of Connecticut similarly charged citizens:

> Finally, ye . . . whose high prerogative it is to . . . invest with office and authority or to withhold them, and in whose power it is to save or destroy your country, consider well the important trust . . . which God . . . [has] put into your hands. To God and posterity you are accountable for them. . . . Let not your children have reason to curse you for giving up those rights, and prostrating those institutions which your fathers delivered to you. [121]

We must be involved; the government of this nation can be blessed only to the extent that we place God-fearing and moral individuals into office. What legacy will we leave the next generation? The choice is ours. ■

Endnotes

1. *Warsaw v. Tehachapi*, No. CV F-90-404 EDP (E.D. Cal. 1990).

2. *Roberts v. Madigan*, 921 F. 2d 1047 (10th Cir. 1990).

3. *Alexander v. Nacogdoches School District*, Civil Action 9: 91CV144 (E.D. Tex. – Lufkin Div. 1991).

4. *Commonwealth v. Chambers*, 599 A. 2d 630, 643-644 (Super. Ct. Pa. 1991).

5. John Locke, *A Collection of Several Pieces of Mr. John Locke* (London: J. Bettenham, 1720), p. A3.

6. Thomas Clarkson, *Memoirs of the Private and Public Life of William Penn* (London: Longman, 1813), Vol. I, p. 303.

7. *The Constitutions of the Several Independent States of America* (Boston: Norman and Bowen, 1785), pp. 99-100, Delaware, 1776, Article 22.

8. *Constitutions*, p. 81, Pennsylvania, 1776, Chapter II, Section 10.

9. *A Constitution or Frame of Government Agreed Upon by the Delegates of the People of the State of Massachusetts-Bay* (Boston: Benjamin Edes & Sons, 1780), p. 44, Chapter VI, Article I.

10. *Constitutions*, p. 138, North Carolina, 1776, Article 32.

11. Benjamin Rush, *A Letter by Dr. Benjamin Rush Describing the Consecration of the German College at Lancaster* (Lancaster, PA: Published by Order of the College, 1945), pp. 9-10.

12. Noah Webster, *History of the United States* (New Haven: Durrie & Peck, 1832), pp. 336-337, ¶ 49.

13. Webster, *History*, p. 337, ¶ 49.

14. Fisher Ames, *Works of Fisher Ames* (Boston: T. B. Wait & Co., 1809), p. 24, Speech on Biennial Elections, January 15, 1788.

15. Benjamin Rush, *Letters of Benjamin Rush*, L. H. Butterfield, editor (Princeton: Princeton University Press, 1951), Vol. I, p. 454, quoting John Joachim Zubly, Presbyterian Pastor and delegate to Congress, in a letter to David Ramsay, March or April, 1788.

16. John Adams, *The Works of John Adams* (Boston: Charles C. Little and James Brown, 1851), Vol. VI, p. 484, to John Taylor, April 15, 1814.

17. Webster, *History*, p. 6.

18. William Blackstone, *Commentaries on the Laws of England* (Philadelphia: Robert Bell, 1771), Four Volumes.

19. Blackstone, *Commentaries*, Vol. I, pp. 42-43.

20. Thomas Jefferson, *Notes on the State of Virginia* (Philadelphia: Matthew Carey, 1794), Query XVIII, p. 237.

21. John Adams, *Papers of John Adams*, Robert J. Taylor, editor (Cambridge: The Belknap Press, 1977), Vol. 1, p. 81, "u" to the Boston Gazette, August 29, 1763.

22. Rush, *Letters*, Vol. I, p. 244, to Charles Lee, October 24, 1779.

23. Benjamin Rush, *Essays, Literary, Moral & Philosophical* (Philadelphia: Thomas and Samuel F. Bradford, 1798), p. 112, "A Defence of the Use of the Bible as a School Book."

24. Robert Ingersoll, *Ingersollia: Gems of Thought from the Lectures, Speeches, and Conversations of Colonel Robert G. Ingersoll* (Chicago: Belford, Clarke, & Co., 1882), pp. 43-44.

25. Ingersoll, *Ingersollia*, p. 49.

26. Abraham Lincoln, *The Collected Works of Abraham Lincoln*, Roy P. Basler, editor (New Brunswick: Rutgers University Press, 1953), Vol. IV, p. 235, address to the New Jersey Senate, February 21, 1861.

27. M. L. Weems, *The Life of George Washington* (Philadelphia: Joseph Allen, 1800), p. 6.

28. Weems, *Life*, pp. 7-8.

29. Thomas Jefferson Wertenbaker, *Princeton: 1746-1896* (Princeton: Princeton University Press, 1946), p. 88; Lawrence A. Cremin, *American Education: The Colonial Experience*, 1607-1783 (New York: Harper & Row, 1970), p. 301; *Nation Under God: A Religious-Patriotic Anthology*, Frances Brentano, editor (Great Neck, NY: Channel Press, 1957), pp. 41-42; Dr. John Eidsmoe, *Christianity and The Constitution* (Grand Rapids: Baker Books, 1987), p. 83; Samuel Davies Alexander, *Princeton College During the Eighteenth Century* (New York: Anson D. F. Randolph & Company, 1872), pp. 121-185.

30. John Witherspoon, *The Works of the Reverend John Witherspoon* (Philadelphia: William W. Woodward, 1802), Vol. III, p. 42.

31. Abigail Adams, *Letters of Mrs. Adams, The Wife of John Adams* (Boston: Charles C. Little and James Brown, 1840), Vol. 1, p. 76, to John Adams, November 5, 1775.

32. John Witherspoon, *The Works of John Witherspoon* (Edinburgh: J. Ogle, 1815), Vol. IV, pp. 266-267, from "A Sermon Delivered at a Public Thanksgiving after Peace."

33. John Adams, *Works*, Vol. II, pp. 293-294.

34. John Adams, *Works*, Vol. II, p. 294.

35. Matthias Burnet, *An Election Sermon, Preached at Hartford, on the Day of the Anniversary Election, May 12, 1803* (Hartford: Hudson & Goodwin, 1803), pp. 7, 9, 16, 27.

36. See, for example, Charles Warren, *Odd Byways in American History* (Cambridge: Harvard University Press, 1942), p. 127; Dumas Malone, *Jefferson and the Ordeal of Liberty* (Boston: Little Brown and Company, 1962), p. 481; and *The William and Mary Quarterly*, Third Series, October 1948, Vol. V, No. 4, "Jefferson and the Election of 1800: A Case Study in the Political Smear," by Charles O. Lerche, Jr., pp. 470, 472.

37. Abigail Adams, *New Letters of Abigail Adams, 1788-1801*, Stewart Mitchell, editor (Boston: Houghton Mifflin Company, 1947), pp. 265-266, to her sister, February 7, 1801.

38. Noah Webster, *Letters to a Young Gentleman Commencing His Education to Which is Subjoined a Brief History of the United States* (New Haven: S. Converse, 1823), p. 18, Letter 1.

39. Webster, *Letters to a Young Gentleman*, pp. 18-19, Letter 1.

40. Burnet, *Election Sermon*, p. 27.

41. Chandler Robbins, *A Sermon Preached Before His Excellency John Hancock, Esq., Governour . . . of the Commonwealth of Massachusetts, May 25, 1791, Being the Day of General Election* (Boston: Thomas Adams, 1791), p. 18.

42. Webster, *Letters to a Young Gentleman*, p. 19, Letter 1.

43. Webster, *Letters to a Young Gentleman*, p. 19, Letter 1.

44. Ingersoll, *Ingersollia*, pp. 49, 50, 52, 54.

45. The first platform for the National Liberal League was published on October 26, 1877. Its platform called for "total separation of church and state"; "taxation of church property"; "abolition of chaplaincies"; etc.

46. The 2000 census established 209 million voting age adults in America; the February 25 to March 10, 2002 Pew Research Center Survey ("2002 Religion and Public Life Survey") indicates that 29 percent of Americans consider themselves "born again, Evan-

gelicals." Therefore, 29 percent of 209 million results in 60 million voting age Americans who would call themselves "born again, Evangelicals." The same Pew Research Survey establishes that over 10 million Evangelicals confess that they are not registered to vote, and an additional 2 million have inadvertently allowed their voter registration to lapse. This indicates that 12 million of the 60 million are not registered to vote, resulting in 20 percent of Evangelicals. The Republican National Committee conducted separate research, comparing lists of church members at Evangelical churches with voter registration files and found that a full 40 percent of Evangelicals were not registered to vote, resulting in a total of 24 million. While this number is almost twice as high as that reached by Pew, the difference in the two numbers can be attributed to suggested reasons such as many Evangelicals are ashamed to say they are not registered when questioned by surveyors.

47. Rush, *Essays*, pp. 10-11, "Of The Mode of Education Proper in a Republic."

48. B. F. Tefft, *The Life of Daniel Webster* (Philadelphia: Porter and Coats, 1854), p. 470.

49. Charles G. Finney, *Lectures on Revivals of Religion* (New York: Fleming H. Revell Company, 1868, originally printed 1835), Lecture XV, pp. 281-282.

50. James A. Garfield, *The Works of James Abram Garfield*, Burke Hinsdale, editor (Boston: James R. Osgood and Company, 1883), Vol. II, pp. 486, 489, "A Century of Congress," July, 1877.

51. US Census Bureau, "*Statistical Abstract of the United States 1990*: No. 297, Child Maltreatment Cases Reported – Summary: 1976 to 1986" (at http://www2.census.gov/prod2/statcomp/documents/1990-01.pdf).

52. Centers for Disease Control and Prevention, "HIV-AIDS Surveillance Report, 2005: Table 3, p. 12; Table 7, pp. 16-17; Table 8, p. 18" (at http://www.cdc.gov/hiv/topics/surveil-lance/resources/reports/2005report/pdf/2005SurveillanceReport.pdf).

53. US Census Bureau, "*The Statistical Abstract*: Table 329, Federal Prosecutions of Public Corruption: 1980 to 2004 (at http://www.census.gov/compendia/statab/tables/07s0329.xls).

54. *Engel v. Vitale*, 370 U.S. 421 (1962).

55. *Abington v. Schempp*; 374 U.S. 203, 220-221 (1963).

56. *Abington v. Schempp*; 374 U.S. 203 (1963).

57. *Abington* at 209.

58. *Stone v. Graham*, 449 U.S. 39 (1980).

59. See, for example, *State v. Mockus*, 113 A. 39, 41 (Me. 1921); *Cason v. Baskin*, 20 So.2d 243, 247 (Fla. 1944) (en banc); *Bertera's Hopewell Foodland, Inc. v. Masters*, 236 A.2d 197, 200-201 (Pa. 1967); *Paramount-Richards Theatres v. City of Hattiesburg*, 49 So.2d 574, 577 (Miss. 1950); *People v. Rubenstein*, 182 N.Y.S.2d 548, 550 (N.Y. Ct. Sp. Sess. 1959); *Stollenwerck v. State*, 77 So. 52, 54 (Ala. Ct. App. 1917) (Brown, P. J., concurring); *Gillooley v. Vaughn*, 110 So. 653, 655 (Fla. 1926) (citing *Theisen v. McDavid*, 16 So. 321, 323 (Fla. 1894)); *Rogers v. State*, 4 S.E.2d 918, 919 (Ga. Ct. App. 1939); *Brimhall v. Van Campen*, 8 Minn. 1 (1858); *City of Ames v. Gerbracht*, 189 N.W. 729, 733 (Iowa 1922); *Sumpter v. State*, 306 N.E.2d 95, 101 (Ind. 1974); *State v. Schultz*, 582 N.W.2d 113, 117 (Wis. Ct. App. 1998); *Ruiz v. Clancy*, 157 So. 737, 738 (La. Ct. App. 1934) (citing *Caldwell v. Henmen*, 5 Rob. 20 (La. 1843)); *Pierce v. Yerkovich*, 363 N.Y.S.2d 403, 414 (N.Y. Fam. Ct. 1974); *Mileski v. Locker*, 178 N.Y.S.2d 911, 916 (N.Y. Sup. Ct. 1958); *Beaty v. McGoldrick*, 121 N.Y.S.2d 431, 432 (N.Y. Sup. Ct. 1953); *Young v. Commonwealth*, 53 S.W. 963, 966 (Ky. Ct. App. 1932); *Ex parte Mei*, 192 A. 80, 82 (N.J. 1937); *Hardin v. State*, 46 S.W. 803, 808 (Tex. Crim. App.

1898); *Schreifels v. Schreifels*, 287 P.2d 1001, 1005 (Wash. 1955); *Barbour v. Barbour*, 330 P.2d 1093, 1098 (Mont. 1958); *Petition of Smith*, 71 F. Supp. 968, 972 (D.N.J. 1947); *S.B. v. S.J.B.*, 609 A.2d 124, 125 (N.J. Super. Ct. Ch. Div. 1992); *Succession of Onorato*, 51 So.2d 804, 810 (La. 1951); *Hollywood Motion Picture Equipment Co. v. Furer*, 105 P.2d 299, 301 (Cal. 1940); *State v. Donaldson*, 99 P. 447, 449 (Utah 1909); *De Rinzie v. People*, 138 P. 1009, 1010 (Colo. 1913); *Addison v. State*, 116 So. 629 (Fla. 1928); *Anderson v. Maddox*, 65 So.2d 299, 301-302 (Fla. 1953); *State v. Gould*, 46 S.W.2d 886, 889-890 (Mo. 1932); *Doll v. Bender*, 47 S.E. 293, 300 (W.Va. 1904) (Dent, J., concurring); *Pennsylvania Co. v. United States*, 214 F. 445, 455 (W.D. Pa. 1914); *Watts v. Gerking*, 228 P. 135, 141 (Or. 1924); *Hosford v. State*, 525 So.2d 789, 799 (Miss. 1988); *People v. Rosen*, 20 Cal.App.2d 445, 448-449, 66 P.2d 1208 (1937); *Pullum v. Johnson*, 647 So.2d 254, 256 (Fla. Dist. Ct. App. 1994); *Weinstock, Lubin & Co. v. Marks*, 42 P. 142, 145 (Cal. 1895); *Chisman v. Moylan*, 105 So.2d 186, 189 (Fla. Dist. Ct. App. 1958); *Swift & Co. v. Peterson*, 233 P.2d 216, 231 (Or. 1951), and others.

60. *Stone v. Graham*, 449 U.S. 39, 42 (1980).

61. AP report from April 6, 1992, from DeFuniak Spring, FL; article taken from *Olean [New York] Times Herald*.

62. Robbins, *A Sermon*, p. 32.

63. James Madison, *The Papers of James Madison*, Henry D. Gilpin, editor (Washington. DC: Langtree & O'Sullivan, 1840), Vol. III, p. 1391, August 22, 1787.

64. *The Debates in the Several State Conventions*, Jonathan Elliot, editor (Washington, DC: Jonathan Elliot, 1836), Vol. I, p. 374, Luther Martin, January 27, 1788.

65. James D. Richardson, *A Compilation of the Messages and Papers of the Presidents*, (Published by Authority of Congress, 1897), Vol. I, p. 45, "First Inaugural Address," April 30, 1789.

66. See the US Census Bureau's *Statistical Abstract of the United States* for the Years 1969, 1980, 1990, & 2007: "Crime and Crime Rates By Type" (at http://www.census.gov/compendia/statab/).

67. US Department of Justice, "Bureau of Justice Statistics: State Prison Expenditures, 2001, p. 2" (at http://www.ojp.usdoj.gov/bjs/pub/pdf/spe01.pdf).

68. National Criminal Justice Reference Service, "Office of Juvenile Justice and Delinquency Prevention: Juvenile Justice Bulletin, November 2002" (at http://www.ncjrs.gov/pdffiles1/ojjdp/191729.pdf).

69. Chapin Hall Center for Children at the University of Chicago, "Too Soon to Tell: Deciphering Recent Trends in Youth Violence: Issue Brief, November 2006" (at http://www.chapinhall.org/article_abstract.aspx?ar=1437).

70. See the US Census Bureau's Statistical Abstract of the United States for the years 1980, 1990, 1991, & 2006: "Births To Unmarried Women" and "Legal Abortions By Selected Characteristics" (at http://www.census.gov/compendia/statab/).

71. Alan Guttmacher Institute, *Family Planning Perspectives*, Vol. 19, No. 2, March/April 1987.

72. US Census Bureau, "Statistical Abstract of the United States 2003: No. HS-14: Births to Teenagers and to Unmarried Women: 1940 to 2002" (at http://www.census.gov/statab/hist/HS-14.pdf).

73. National Campaign to Prevent Teen Pregnancy, "By the Numbers: The Public Costs of Teen Childbearing, October 2006" (at www.teenpregnancy.org/costs/pdf/report/ BTN National Report.pdf).

74. See, as just one indication, incidents of syphilis: American Sexually Transmitted Diseases Association, "Epidemiology of Syphilis in the United States, 1941-1993: Age distribution of primary and secondary syphilis by gender, United States, 1956, 1979, 1990, and 1993" (at http://www.stdjournal.com/pt/re/std/fulltext.00007435-199601000-00006. htm;jsessionid=GnVJbTLMJX4HyDhv7p6nBTxyfJkJ3GRL9wMWtXVpsfWZnwJpJ-Phy!3145886!-949856145!8091!-1?index=1&database=ppvovft&results=1&count=10&se archid=7&nav=search). There are literally dozens of separate sexually transmitted diseases that show similar rises to previously unrecorded highs.

75. David Barton, *America: To Pray or Not To Pray?* (Aledo, TX: WallBuilder Press, 1994), pp. 26, 31, 33, 51-53, 88, 98-104, data obtained from Department of Health and Human Services; the *Statistical Abstracts of the United States*; The Center for Disease Control; *Family Planning Perspectives*, March/April 1987; *Sexual and Reproductive Behavior of American Women*, 1982-88, furnished by the Alan Guttmacher Institute; US National Center for Health Statistics, *Vital Statistics of the United States*, annual; Department of Commerce, Census Bureau; *National Study on Child Neglect and Abuse Reporting*, annual, provided by American Humane Association, Denver, CO; *AIDS Weekly Surveillance Report – United States*, Center for Disease Control; *National Survey of Drug Abuse*, provided by National Institute on Drug Abuse; University of Michigan Survey, *Reader's Digest*, August 1983, p. 138; and many, many other post-1963 governmental sources.

76. John Dickinson, *The Political Writings of John Dickinson* (Wilmington: Bonsal and Niles, 1801), Vol. I, p. 277, quoting from Baron de Montesquieu, *Spirit of the Laws* (Philadelphia: Isaiah Thomas, 1802), Vol. I, p. 272.

77. William Jay, *The Life of John Jay* (New York: J. & J. Harper, 1833), Vol. II, p. 376, to John Murray, Jr., October 12, 1816.

78. John Jay, *The Correspondence and Public Papers of John Jay* (New York: G. P. Putnam's Sons, 1893), Vol. IV, p. 365, to Rev. Dr. Morse, January 1, 1813.

79. II Chronicles 19:1-2.

80. George Washington, *Address of George Washington, President of the United States, and Late Commander in Chief of the American Army, to the People of the United States, Preparatory to His Declination* (Baltimore: Christopher Jackson, 1796), pp. 19-20.

81. David Ramsay, *An Eulogium upon Benjamin Rush, M. D.* (Philadelphia: Bradford and Inskeep, 1813), p. 103.

82. Ramsay, *Eulogium*, p. 103.

83. See, for example, *Board of Airport Commissioners v. Jews for Jesus*, 482 U.S. 569 (1987).

84. *Harper v. Poway Unified School District*, No. 04-57037 (9th Cir. 2006); Los Angeles Times, "Free-speech fashion" (at http://www.latimes.com/news/opinion/editorials/la-ed-tshirt26apr26,0,1795156.story); *The Washington Times*, "Pro-lifers suited to a T" (at http://www.washingtontimes.com/culture/20040426-102738-6978r.htm); World Net Daily, "Students suspended for 'anti-gay' shirts'" (at http://wnd.com/news/article. asp?ARTICLE ID=50016), and "Pro-life shirt equated with swastika" (at http://www. worldnetdaily.com/news/article.asp?ARTICLE ID=30781); Connection Magazine, "Who

would say a Christian Pro-Life T-shirt was the same as a Nazi Swastika?" (at http://www. connectionmagazine.org/2003_04/ts_prolife_tshirt.htm).

85. *Draper v. Logan County Public Library*, 2005 WL 3358686 (W.D. Ky. Aug. 29, 2003).

86. *Steiger v. Lord-Larson*, No. 05-C-0700-S (W.D. Wis. Mar. 2006); The Badger Herald, "Campus dorm policy under review" (at http://badgerherald.com/news/2005/11/10/campus_dorm_policy_u.php).

87. *Evelyn M. Shatkin & Linda Shifflett v. University of Texas at Arlington, et. al.*, No. 4:06-CV882Y (N.D. Tex. 2006); CBN News, "Were Women Fired for Praying at Work?" (at http://www.cbn.com/CBNnews/75589.aspx).

88. *Anderson v. Milwaukee County*, 433 F.3d 975 (7th Cir. 2006).

89. *Murphy v. Zoning Commission of the Town of New Milford*, 289 F. Supp. 2d. 87 (D.Conn. 2003).

90. *Konikov v. Orange County*, 410 F.3d 1317 (11th Cir. 2005); *Town of Foxfield v. Archdiocese of Denver*, 2006 WL 2291160 (Colo. Ct. App. Aug. 10, 2006).

91. See *Furley v. Aledo Independent School District* No. 4:99-CV-0416-A (N.D. Tex. Oct. 21, 1999), *aff'd without opinion*, 218 F.3d 743 (5th Cir. 2000); *Corpus Christi Caller Times*, "5th Circuit dismisses case of edited graduation prayer" (at http://www.coastalbendhealth.com/2000/may/31/today/texas_me/1336.html); also *Amarillo Globe-News*, "School district gets sued over prayer policy" (at www.amarillo.com/stories/052999/tex_LD0623.002.shtml), and "Court of appeals dismisses school prayer case" (at www.amarillo.com/stories/053100/tex_LD0634.shtml); also Levitt Letter, "October 1999, Volume 21, Number 10: Standing ovation for taking a stand on faith" (at http://www.levitt.com/newsletters/1999-10.html); *Hinricks v. Bosma* (S.D. Ind. 2006); *Hinrichs v. Bosma*, Nos. 05-4604 and 05-4781 (7th Cir. 2006); *Jane Doe v. Santa Fe Independent School District*, No. G-95-176 (S.D. Tex. 1995) (court transcription of verbal ruling by federal judge Samuel Kent, pp. 3-4); *Doe v. Tangipahoa Parish School Board*, No. 05-30294 (5th Cir. 2006); *Hashmel Turner v. The City Council of the City of Fredericksburg, Virginia* (E.D. Va. Aug.3, 2006).

92. *Freda Brown v. First Baptist Church of Dallas Texas*, No. 306CV1853 (N.D. Tex. Oct. 10, 2006); Dallas Morning News, "Teacher accusing First Baptist of bias" (at http://www.dallasnews.com/sharedcontent/dws/dn/latestnews/stories/101306metbaptist.35bd025.html#).

93. *Westbrook v. Penley, & Doe v. Watermark Church*, 146 S.W.3d 220 (Tex. App. 2004), pet. filed No. 04-0838 (Tex. 2006).

94. *H.E.B. Ministries v. Texas Higher Education Coordinating Board*, 114 S.W.3d 617 (Tex. App. 2003), petition for review filed, briefing on the merits requested, No. 03-0995 (Tex. 2004).

95. *Jirtle v. Town of Briscoe*, 175 N.C. App 178 (N.C. 2005).

96. *Living Waters Bible Church, et al. v. Town of Enfield*, No. 01 CV-00450-M (N.H. 2002); *Vacaville Seventh Day Adventist Church and Maranatha Broadcasting v. Solano County, et al.*, Case No. 02-CV-336 (E.D. Cal. 2004).

97. *Fifth Avenue Presbyterian Church v. The City of New York*, 293 F.3d 570 (2d Cir. 2002).

98. *Okemos Christian Center v. Meridian Charter Township*, No. 05-2309 (6th Cir. 2007); *Living Water Church of God v. Charter Twp.* 384 F. Supp. 2d 1123 (W.D. Mich. 2005).

99. *Barr v. City of Sinton*, No. 13-03-00727-CV, 2005 Tex. App. LEXIS 9847 (Tex. Ct. App. Nov. 23, 2005), *petition for review granted*, No. 06-0074 (Tex. 2006).

100. *Men of Destiny Ministries v. County of Osceola*, 6:06-CV-624-ORL-31DAB (M.D. Fla. 2006).

101. *Congregation Kol Ami v. Abington Township*, 309 F.3d 120 (3d Cir. 2002); *Cottonwood Christian Center v. City of Cypress*, 218 F. Supp. 2d 1203 (C.D. Cal. 2002); *Victory Family Life Church v. Douglas County*, No. 04CV01469 (Super. Ct. Douglas County, Ga., Sept. 20, 2005); etc.

102. *Peck v. Baldwinsville Central School District* No. 99-CV-1847(NAM/GJD) (N.D.N.Y. 2000).

103. *Settle v. Dickson County School Board*, 53 F.3d 152 (6th Cir. 1995).

104. *Doe v. South Iron R-1 School District*, No. 4:06-cv-00392 (E.D. Mo. 2006) and No. 06-3373 (8th Cir. Mo. 2006); Liberty Counsel, "School Admits Error and Allows Student To Give Bibles To His Friends" (at http://lc.org/pressrelease/2007/nr022107.htm).

105. *Heinkel v. School Board of Lee County*, 194 Fed. Appx. 604 (11th Cir. 2006); *M.B. v. Liverpool Central School District*, No. 5:04-CV-1255 (NAM/GHL) (N.D.N.Y. 2004); *Cumana v. Bucelo*, No. 99-2107-CIV-JORDAN (S.D. Fla. May 24, 2002); [Morgan] *Nyman/Liberty Counsel, et al. v. School District of Kettle Moraine* (case settled without litigation); *Westfield High School L.I.F.E. Club v. City of Westfield*, 2003 WL 1339052 (D. Mass. Mar. 17, 2003); First Amendment Center, "Student sues N.Y. district for barring religious message" (at http://www.firstamendmentcenter.org/news.aspx?id=14281) Student Press Law Center, "Fla. college ends prior review" (at http://www.splc.org/report_detail.asp?id=863&edition=22); Freedomforum.org, "Wisconsin school board: Girl may hand out religious cards" (at http://www.freedomforum.org/templates/document.asp?documentID=14741); *Milwaukee Journal Sentinel*, "School rejected girl's religious cards, suit says" (at http://www2.jsonline.com/news/wauk/mar01/relig22032101a.asp) and "Board allows religious Valentine's Day cards" (at http://www2.jsonline.com/news/wauk/aug01/valen29082801a.asp).

106. *Curran v. School Board of Broward County*, No. 0460032 (S.D. Fla. Feb. 2005); Student Press Law Center, "Fla. school district settles suit with student who challenged distribution policy" (at http://www.splc.org/newsflash_archives.asp?id=950&year=2005).

107. *Castle Hills First Baptist Church v. City of Castle Hills*, No. SA-01-CA-1149-HG (W.D. Tex. 2003-2004); *Dunamis Community and Outreach Ministries, Inc., v. County of Volusia*, No. 6:01-CV-643-ORL-28-DAB (M.D. Fla. 2002); Liberty Counsel, "Pennsylvania Church No Longer Left Out In The Cold" (at http://www.lc.org/pressrelease/2006/nr120806.htm); Law.com, "Christian Church Wins Right to Build in Spiritualist Community" (at http://www.law.com/jsp/article.jsp?id=1032128628006); *Los Angeles Times*, "Churches Putting Town Out of Business" (at http://www.latimes.com/news/nationworld/nation/la-na-churches31jul31,0,6286040.story?coll=la-home-nation).

108. *Oxford Baptist Church v. Catawba County Schools Board of Education*, No. 5:02-CV-114-V (W.D. N.C. September 9, 2004); *DiLoreto v. Board of Education*, 87 Cal.Rptr.2d 791 (1999).

109. Liberty Counsel, "News Release: Virginia County Bucking Against Cowboy Church" (at http://www.lc.org/pressrelease/2006/nr051006.htm).

110. *Hood v. Keller*, 341 F.3d 593 (6th Cir. 2003).

111. Paul Wallace, *The Muhlenbergs of Pennsylvania* (Philadelphia: University of Pennsylvania Press, 1950), p. 118.

112. Wallace, *Muhlenbergs*, p. 118.

113. Wallace, *Muhlenbergs*, pp. 118-119; see also J. T. Headley, *The Chaplains and Clergy of the Revolution* (Springfield, MA: G. & F. Bill, 1861), pp. 123-124.

114. See, for example, Headley, *Chaplains and Clergy;* Franklin Cole, *They Preached Liberty* (New York: Fleming H. Revell, 1941); Daniel Dorchester, *Christianity in the United States from the First Settlement Down to the Present Time* (New York: Phillips & Hunt, 1888); Alice M. Baldwin, *The New England Clergy and the American Revolution* (New York: Frederick Ungar, 1958); John Wingate Thornton, *Pulpit of the American Revolution* (Boston: Gould and Lincoln, 1860); *The Patriot Preachers of the American Revolution* (Printed for the Subscribers, 1860); etc.

115. Wallace, *Muhlenbergs*, p. 121.

116. Wallace, *Muhlenbergs*, pp. 120-121.

117. Madison, *Papers*, Vol. III, p. 1324, by John Francis Mercer, August 14, 1787.

118. Madison, *Papers*, Vol. III, p. 1324, by John Francis Mercer, August 14, 1787.

119. John Adams, *Works*, Vol. IX, p. 229, to the Officers of the First Brigade of the Third Division of the Militia of Massachusetts, October 11, 1798.

120. Finney, *Lectures*, Lecture XV, pp. 281-282.

121. Burnet, *Election Sermon*, pp. 26-27.

Also Available from WallBuilders

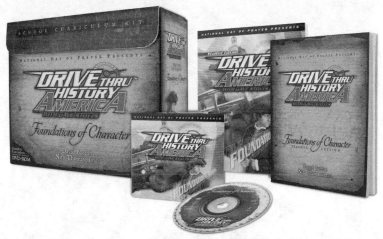

A history curriculum that unabashedly delivers the truth!
Drive Through History America
written by David Barton & presented by award-winning actor Dave Stotts

Visit our website for other great resources!

800-873-2845 • www.wallbuilders.com